HOMO
DONGMICUS

The Evolution *from an*
Office Worker
↳ *to an* **Influence**

HOMO
DONGMICUS

The Evolution from an —
Office Worker
to an
Influence

초판 1쇄 발행 2024. 2. 9.

지은이 Sarah Dongmi Choi
펴낸이 김병호
펴낸곳 주식회사 바른북스

편집진행 Dongock Choe, Jeremy On
디자인 W+East Creative Studio

등록 2019년 4월 3일 제2019-000040호
주소 서울시 성동구 연무장5길 9-16, 301호 (성수동2가, 블루스톤타워)
대표전화 070-7857-9719 | **경영지원** 02-3409-9719 | **팩스** 070-7610-9820

•바른북스는 여러분의 다양한 아이디어와 원고 투고를 설레는 마음으로 기다리고 있습니다.

이메일 barunbooks21@naver.com | **원고투고** barunbooks21@naver.com
홈페이지 www.barunbooks.com | **공식 블로그** blog.naver.com/barunbooks7
공식 포스트 post.naver.com/barunbooks7 | **페이스북** facebook.com/barunbooks7

HOMO DONGMICUS

The Evolution from an office Worker to an Influencer

Sarah Dongmi Choi

CREATE YOUR STORY
CONNECT YOUR WORLD
BUILD YOUR BRAND!

바른북스

Prologue

After reaching 8,000 followers on LinkedIn, I headed to COEX, Korea's largest exhibition hall, for NextRise, a global startup event.

Nervous but excited, I aimed to network actively. As the person in charge of investments and the global expansion of startups for my company, this was a great opportunity.

As soon as I entered, I started scanning attendees' name badges and approached a venture capitalist. Before I could even give him my business card, he said,

"Huh, it's you, I saw you on LinkedIn!"

"It is! Nice to meet you." I replied.

We briefly chatted, and I was about to leave when another person approached me and asked for a picture together. I snapped the photo, tagged him, posted it to LinkedIn, and guess what? Three people responded to my LinkedIn post asking where I was, came over, sat down, and exchanged business cards.

That week, my LinkedIn posts received a staggering 85,000 views, which was a new milestone for me at the time.

At that moment, I realized I had indeed become an established influencer. I no longer had to introduce myself to people, and they were excited to meet me and converse well beyond the digital space. Growing your brand on LinkedIn not only sets you up for success on the platform but wherever you go.

As of 2023, LinkedIn boasts more than 3 million subscribers in Korea. The business networking platform used by 950 million people in 200 countries has a growing presence on the Asian peninsula. (Source: LinkedIn)

In Korea, recruitment professionals and global company employees embraced LinkedIn in its early stages.

Since then, professional groups in human resources, marketing, and IT have begun using the platform to enhance their expertise by sharing knowledge. Company sales reps are also active on LinkedIn, seizing global business opportunities.

I wrote this book to share how I gained 10,000 followers on LinkedIn as a startup and investment content creator and to chart my growth as a micro-influencer.

Micro-influencers with 1,000 to 100,000 followers are relatively small compared to "Mega-influencers" with 100,000 to 1 million followers, but they have a strong voice within their niche communities.

Any office worker or business owner can become a

micro-influencer; all you need to do is put in some effort. You can leverage your influence in your industry and community to gain professional knowledge and build your business network.

If you've specialized in a field for over three years, you can harness your knowledge and experience to create content.

Being an influencer in your field can keep your professional network well-informed, boosting productivity and efficiency in your work and organization.

Suppose you want to be famous in your industry. In that case, you need to network strategically and get the attention of key industry figures. A prolific LinkedIn presence can establish you as a trusted expert, which can also help your company or organization gain traction.

I've seen firsthand that anyone can create content based on expertise. LinkedIn makes it easy to achieve personal branding goals. My experiences and desire to help others inspired me to write this book.

In this book, I'll show you how I succeeded in personal branding as a startup and investment professional through two years of LinkedIn activity and content creator challenges.

I encourage individuals and businesses to take on the challenge of branding themselves on the global platform of LinkedIn, as personal growth can directly benefit business operations.

The book also includes stories from LinkedIn influencers in their respective fields of expertise who are key members of my network and offer incredible insights. I want to thank my friends on LinkedIn for their generous sharing of their stories.

Table of Contents

Global Startup Ecosystem Builders

Content Creators

Global Networking Professionals

Epilogue

Part 1

Sarah Dongmi Choi: Remember the Name

It all starts with an eight-letter word: LinkedIn

In August 2021, I was immersed in my job. Working with startups was exciting, and I always felt a sense of accomplishment after planning and executing a new project, so I was constantly designing and implementing new things. But there was a problem.

I enjoyed working at my company and interacting with startup founders and other stakeholders. Still, when I interacted with those outside my company, it would take me minutes to explain what I did or the organization I belonged to. With limited time to introduce or explain myself, I often ended up exchanging business cards without even being able to present my work - much less knowing if the other party even understood what I did or not.

What made this problem worse was that many people in the narrow startup ecosystem had yet to know who I was.

I thought,

'I've been working really hard for seven years... So why do so many people not know who I am - even in my own startup space?'

In the startup world, no matter what you do, your network is everything. To attract follow-up investments from the startups my company invested in, we had to increase our contacts with venture capitalists. Networking with startups' PR and marketing contacts was crucial for raising early-stage investments. In recent years, global connections have become increasingly important as startups need to go global.

LinkedIn is where all of these people are concentrated, and advances in technology will only continue to make LinkedIn's presence stronger. So, one day, I decided to log on to my long-dormant LinkedIn account. I had a thought:

'Why don't I give LinkedIn a try?'

Goal: Get 100 LinkedIn followers

I've always valued my connections, so I have quite a few business cards. Today, I have over 4,000 online business cards, which means I've already surpassed the "King of the Networking Universe" status awarded by one business card app.

First, I entered the email information of my business cards into my email account "Contacts" list. LinkedIn has an import feature for email accounts, so I immediately requested to be connected to my connections on LinkedIn.

Since I already had a one-on-one relationship with these contacts and only about 10% of my business cards were on LinkedIn, I started with 100 valuable connections.

It can be a bit daunting to start from zero when you first join LinkedIn. So, if you create an account, start with at least 50 to 100 connections using LinkedIn's email-linking function.

If you don't have a lot of contacts or want to start a new network, don't worry; LinkedIn has a feature that suggests connections based on a user's profile and work history.

Suppose you click on the "Connections" section at the top of the first page. In that case, you'll be presented with recommendations based on profile analysis and connections algorithms, such as "People who live in South Korea," "Graduated from Seoul National University," "Technology, Information, Internet," "Groups you might be interested in," and more.

Now, let's get your first 100 LinkedIn connections.

How to increase your acceptance rate on LinkedIn

There are a lot of ways to increase your acceptance rate on LinkedIn, but there are four tips that are non-negotiable:

- **Profile picture**

A profile picture that captures the vibe of your field can go a long way in expanding your network. For example, if you work in IT, you might wear a casual T-shirt. If you work in the legal or sales field, a professional outfit like a suit helps to convey your professionalism. A profile picture that fits your industry or job function will help you feel comfortable and familiar when networking, which will help your networking efforts.

Recently, there have been many AI-imaging apps that can transform one's outfits and hairstyles, giving more freedom to create a desired image.

I went to a photo studio to take my profile picture. It's a good idea to go with a family member, friend, or someone who naturally makes you smile. A big smile on your profile connotes positive energy and will make a good impression on more people.

- **Business logos and pages**

If your profile picture is the first thing someone sees when accepting a connection, they're likely to look at the logo and company name of your organization.

Suppose your current company has a logo and page on LinkedIn. In that case, you'll have an easier time getting an acceptance. If your company is not yet on LinkedIn and you don't have a company account, I recommend talking to your marketing department about creating a company page. If you don't actually know someone and they don't have a profile picture or a company logo, they're less likely to accept your request.

Remember that a blank logo and page won't convince the people you want to get connected with.

- **A headline that makes an impact**

One of the trickiest parts of crafting a LinkedIn page is creating a headline. But if you make sure to include the following, you'll be well on your way to connecting with more people in your desired industry:

1) Your area of expertise

2) Your career aspirations

3) The industry you're interested in connecting with

I've been tweaking my headline for two years as I've changed projects. If I change my career scope in the future, I will likely change my headline again. My current headlines look like this.

Do it Now! | Tech Startup Accelerator in South Korea | +10K LinkedIn Influencer | 2023 e27 Woman Top 10 Contributor | Startup Ecosystem Content Creator | Global Entrepreneurship | Connecting the dots

If you need help with what to write, start by looking at examples of people in similar roles in the same industry to help you craft your own unique headline.

- **Link to a webpage that showcases your strengths**

Below your LinkedIn profile is a space for one additional link. This can be a link to your blog, social media profiles, or anything else you'd like to give your future connections more information about what you do and who you are.

The only caveat is that if the linked webpage is incomplete, this strategy can backfire. If your LinkedIn page contains poorly made links or little content, you may be better off not putting links in your profile.

To demonstrate my global reach as a startup expert, I included a link to my "About" page on the international startup-investor platform e27.

Clicking on this link will take you to my English bio and two current articles as a "Thought Leader."

Goal: Get 500 LinkedIn followers

There's a reason why the number "500" is so essential on LinkedIn. When you meet with clients or investors overseas, they often ask for your LinkedIn QR code instead of your business card. Sometimes, business relationships and investment considerations are based on whether or not you have 500 connections on LinkedIn. This is because 500 connections can give the impression of a "capable, well-connected" professional with the right amount of industry connections - not too many, not too few.

A business page with more than 500 followers can

also give the impression that the company is somewhat established in the industry.

I took a lot of time to strategically create my 500 connections because this number will be the blueprint for how I will network on LinkedIn.

"Who are the people in my field?"
"Who are the people in my future trending areas?"
"Who are the influencers in my field?"

I kept asking myself these questions and slowly and carefully built my network. Of course, not everyone will be willing to accept your connection requests, so if you want to expand your network in a particular field, send out lots of connection requests!

LinkedIn also creates a domino effect of sorts. If you find someone who is active on LinkedIn with a robust network and has a well-crafted profile, it's worth sending them a short, straightforward introduction and mentioning possible future collaborations. You'll have a much better chance of getting accepted. If you make good connections early on, you'll have a quality network when you grow to 1,000 or 5,000 connections.

People are always looking for forward-thinking networks. If someone looks you up and all your connections are people they know, you will appear insular and unwilling to branch out. I recommend a 70/30 ratio of people in your field and people in other areas.

You can only have up to 30,000 connections on LinkedIn, but there is no limit to the number of followers you can have. The more connections you have, the likelihood of connecting with people in your desired industry increases exponentially.

Above all, be diligent in sending out connection requests to build a network of 500 connections, demonstrating professionalism and credibility.

It's About Who You Know - Not What You Know

• **I don't know who you are, but let's talk**

With a well-written LinkedIn profile, you're more likely to get connected with local and international professionals and companies with more business opportunities. Since I've put much effort into my LinkedIn profile, I get one or two weekly meeting requests from global startup-related companies.

If you're asked to meet, try a coffee chat (a casual online or offline meeting) first. Without the hassle or pressure of traveling to a meeting location and meeting in person, online coffee chats are a common practice among users. It can be more efficient if you ask for the purpose of the meeting and relevant materials in advance.

I often receive requests for coffee chats from people in various fields, and I accept them when possible. Through these meetings, I have found business partners and met extraordinary people who support and encourage each other. In part 7 of this book, I share stories of professionals in various fields I have met through LinkedIn connections.

- **Don't be Shy!**

The future is an era of hyper-convergence. LinkedIn is full of forward-thinking people who are preparing for the future.

LinkedIn is a platform that allows you to connect with people in industries and fields that are expected to grow in the future, even if they are not relevant to you today.

I'm connected to a wide range of experts from around the world in Sustainability, AI, NFTs, and the Metaverse. Through an interview, I wrote an article about a generative AI expert. I also learned about globalization and localization from a Silicon Valley startup expert who visited Korea.

You can get a lot of information from your LinkedIn connections in high-growth business areas, so it's important to keep networking outside your comfort zone.

I've always craved connections to new worlds and future-focused people. With a treasure trove of links just a search and a click away, LinkedIn is a great place to connect with these people and create business opportunities.

- **How Synergy is more Important than a Workplace Buzzword**

I work for an accelerator company that incubates and invests in startups. As a result, I connected with startup professionals from various countries, including the US, China, Hong Kong, Singapore, and Europe.

In particular, Singaporeans and Hong Kongers have a

wealth of experience in various markets across Asia, the US, and Europe, so it's essential to connect with people from these financial and trade hubs.

Connecting with a celebrity or influencer in your industry can make it easier to expand your network later on. Don't hesitate to reach out to these connections. I once asked a Silicon Valley investor featured on TV to connect with me, and he accepted the request in less than five minutes.

However, as you can imagine, some people you want to connect with are picky about who they accept, so if you wish such people to accept your connection requests, it's a good idea to be polite and concise in your introduction. I can't stress enough that a well-crafted profile is a must.

Part 2.

Going Up the Food Chain: From a Small Minnow to a Big Fish

Goal: Get 1,000 LinkedIn followers

"1,000" is a significant number on LinkedIn. When you hit 1,000 followers, you'll be eligible for Creator status.

Once you become a LinkedIn Creator, you can add topics to your profile, host LinkedIn Live or audio events, and publish newsletters. These resources are great ways to deepen relationships with your followers and gain new ones.

LinkedIn Live is hosted by creators worldwide, and if you schedule your sessions ahead of time, followers will get a notification when they commence so that they can join your sessions in real time.

If you have 500 followers, you're likely to hit 1,000 in as little as four weeks and as long as 10 weeks. People prioritize connecting with people with more than 1,000 followers. If you want to connect with more people, try to reach 1,000 followers first.

Reaching this number gives me confidence and a strong motivation to connect with more people.

Remember that 1,000 followers make you a micro-influencer, so don't stop applying and posting until you reach that number.

The 1,000-follower Milestone

You will be proud of reaching the 1,000-follower mark, but it's also the stage where you'll see a dramatic increase in your acceptance rate. If 500 is the number that shows your expertise and credibility in your industry, 1,000 is the number that shows your "influence" with users.

If you have 1,000 connections with 50 followers, you're now exposing your presence and content to over 50,000 people.

I often organize online seminars for my company on

how to take startups global or raise investment. One of my biggest concerns is recruiting participants. However, after reaching 1,000 followers, this was no longer an issue.

I asked my connections in the bio-healthcare industry to spread the news of an event I was promoting, and they were happy to help. Since I already have a lot of contacts in the field, I was quickly able to recruit more than 100 participants. The most significant change was that I could easily promote the program without spending money on advertising.

It's also important to remember that real influencers on LinkedIn are those who actively create and post content, not just those with a few connections. It's also worth remembering that active posting will increase your LinkedIn presence.

1,000 people is not a small number. However, the results of attaining this number will be more than you could have ever imagined. They will bring confidence to anyone you reach.

Sarah's Secret Recipe: Collaboration

The influencers I've become friends with are not only known for their diverse and influential content but also for their life wisdom and humor. Through their posts and comments, people can experience comfort and overcome loneliness.

These warm-hearted influencers rejoice with you when good things happen and provide comfort and laughter with their humorous comments when things get tough. Sometimes, when things don't work out as expected, I lose motivation. Still, interacting with these people has given me the inspiration to write and post again.

Also, LinkedIn has a powerful algorithm that gives your posts visibility, and the more "likes" you get, the more visibility your posts will have. When influencers like your posts, they will be seen by these influencers' connections, which means more people will be aware of your content and your presence.

Find like-minded people through active communication, as you'll enjoy collaborating online and growing together. Through LinkedIn, being in different countries and time zones doesn't matter.

Collaborating - That's What Friends are for!

Once you've connected with the right people on LinkedIn, here's how you can be more active and collaborative, exposing you to more users and growing your online presence:

- **More Posts, More People!**

When you post, you can tag users in your posts or upload photos, such as "@Sarah Dongmi Choi."

This is useful if you've taken a photo together or are writing about something related, as it allows your followers to see the name and page of the person you've tagged. If someone tagged you, showing appreciation by commenting, liking, and reposting is a great way to strengthen your relationships with your LinkedIn friends.

- **That's so Punny!**

Some people on LinkedIn write humorous or thoughtful comments. They may visit your page to see what you say, or they may like your post because they like short, witty comments on your posts.

Even if you don't interact with followers directly, LinkedIn is a humanizing place where you can empathize with others, laugh with them, and be comforted by their interactions. The "Like" button is subdivided into six facial expressions. Don't forget to choose the right one for your mood and situation.

- **Piggybacking on Others**

If you want your posts to be seen by more people, you can ask your friends and influencers to repost them.

In fact, I have a lot of connections in the biotech and investment space, so when I come across a post with good information or insights or an event that needs to recruit participants, I can help and get help from them. Don't forget to leave a thank you message or a comment if you find a post helpful - gratitude goes a long way!

- **Coffee Chats - More Than Just Caffeine**

Coffee chats are all the rage on LinkedIn. LinkedIn users meet online or offline to chat about mutual interests and post about them.

Coffee chats are a good way to connect with other LinkedIn users, but they're also a great way to get attention for your posts. My final recommendation is to post a Coffee Chat review to increase your network and grow your follower count.

Webtoon drawn by my LinkedIn friends

#W+EASTOON
- SARAH DONGMI CHOI -

Sarah Dongmi Choi, a 10k+ LinkedIn influencer,

is in charge of an accelerator
linkage at various startup investments.

Sometimes such influencers
try to connect on LinedIn.

While exchanging introductions,
she sent me her introductory video.

Since the video greatly inspired me,

it led me to try
making a video where I speak in English.

Of course I felt embarrassed at the video I made..

Additionally,

she kindly taught me various things.
I appreciate her!

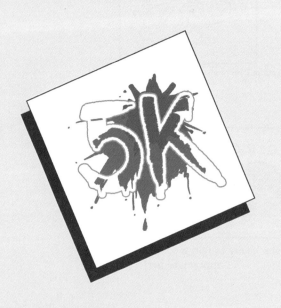

Goal: Get 5,000 LinkedIn followers

A great way to increase your connections in a short amount of time is to create an excellent profile and establish a strong LinkedIn presence. It's great if you have a lot of followers who want to connect with you. However, it can be challenging to increase your followers, so if you want to reach 5,000 followers, you'll need to be proactive with your requests.

I found the right content that resonated with people by experimenting with different post styles. By checking data provided by LinkedIn, I found my style and follower base. In the end, analytics was a crucial part of reaching 5,000 followers.

So, how often should you post to help you get there? Once you have 1,000 followers, one weekly post is enough to reach many people.

Even while sleeping, your posts will continue using their algorithms to reach your immediate circle and promote you. Try to post one piece of content per week, whether it's an article, a photo, or something else.

And, set aside 30 minutes, two days a week, to reach out to the connections you want to increase and those who like you.

Sounds too easy? Keep in mind that only those who take action will reach the 5,000 mark.

TIP 4

Image is Everything

LinkedIn is different from other platforms such as Facebook and Instagram in that it's used by professionals and people who have a specific goal in mind - a career or business opportunity. Posts that project a professional image can be one of your biggest weapons when gaining followers quickly.

- **Be Your Best-Self**

People respond best to photos that show you in your field. Posting photos of yourself at work-related events, post-event group shots, business trips, and other activities that align with your current profile and career path can go a long way toward establishing your credibility as an industry expert.

I work in the startup industry, where networking is vital, so I often attend events and training sessions. When I started posting photos from these events, I got a lot of contacts from startups and investors both locally and abroad.

If you're traveling for work or business, take a moment to post a photo of yourself smiling. A smile is a great way to make a good impression and grow your follower count.

If you meet your LinkedIn connections in person, tagging them can be a great way to get your posts in front of more people.

- **Taking Baby Steps: Using Articles**

Whether in the renewable energy, biotech, IT, marketing, startup, or investment industries, you can easily connect with people worldwide who are in your field if you consistently create posts based on expertise.

Every day, your LinkedIn feed is filled with user posts about industry news, leadership insights, and more. As you connect with people in your industry, the information they post will be useful in your professional life.

When sharing knowledge about specialties, people often post photos of events they've attended or reviews of business trips they've taken, which gives them a sense of immediacy, professionalism, and insight. Many users click the "Like" button.

Even if you write in Korean, LinkedIn has an automatic translation function, which is very useful. It's not perfect, but people will understand what you're saying.

To make a long story short, actively posting your expertise and experience in the form of articles will help to increase your connections and followers.

At first, I didn't post about my work knowledge because I thought I wouldn't contribute any insights. However, each person's experience is different, even in the same field, so when I shared my experiences and insights in posts, people often looked at them differently.

If you have more than three years of work experience, don't hesitate to start posting about your work. You'll have the opportunity to connect with more people and grow.

- **Show what you know!**

LinkedIn is full of people who are thinking about their future, whether they're marketing their businesses or growing their careers. From interns to people with decades of experience, many share insights into their work life, and posts based on social and business experiences are popular.

A post with advice on work-life from someone with a professional background can get hundreds of likes, sometimes over 1,000. Posts about leadership and motivation are also a favorite among users.

Some people have even become best-selling authors by compiling their LinkedIn and social media posts into books (which I aim for!). Don't hesitate to share insights related to your career or expertise.

I've posted about things I've tried my best to accomplish, as well as my resolutions to strategically challenge myself, and I've gotten great responses from users.

Whether it's a story about trial and error or finding a new goal, there's no shortage of material that can resonate with the millions of people out there who are doing the best they can right now.

5,000 followers? Now what?

I met a startup investor at a seminar. We talked about LinkedIn, and she asked me how many connections I had.

"About 5,000."

"Oh, so you're an influencer!"

5,000 seemed tiny since most famous bloggers and YouTubers have at least 100,000 or 1 million followers.

But she explained that if you have that many followers on LinkedIn, you can be called an influencer.

"Me, an influencer?"

That's when I started using the word "influencer."

People I already knew on LinkedIn seemed more interested in me. I started interacting with users through comments and messages.

What was unusual was that I started to see a strange phenomenon: almost everyone I asked to be connected with accepted.

I would go to startup and investment events and give out my business card, and during those moments, I would often hear, "Oh, she's the person from LinkedIn."

After exchanging greetings, people often asked me to take a picture with them and tag them.

I'm not a national celebrity, but it's not as hard as you think to get your name and face out there in your field.

Once I reached 5,000 followers, the time it took me to introduce myself went from a few minutes to just 10 seconds. It was a huge change, and I was ready to move on to another goal.

Now… It's time to aim for 10,000 followers!

Part 3.

LinkedIn Influencer Reborn

User with 5,000 followers?
No, influencer!

You can find people on LinkedIn with as little as 2,000 or 3,000 followers who have become immensely popular because of their powerful messages. Their posts get 100, sometimes 300+ likes and dozens of comments. These are the influencers that LinkedIn users literally love.

Most of you reading this book are more interested in building your brand, expanding your network, and becoming influencers in your field and adjacent fields than reaching 10,000 followers.

However, given that the reach of your posts is statistically more likely to be limited to the number of followers you have, having 5,000 followers will give you more influence in absolute numbers. Even if it seems a little far away and challenging, I encourage you to keep trying until you reach the 5,000 mark.

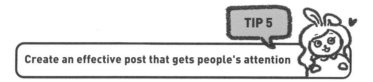

As a first-time poster, I tried a lot of different things. Thankfully, LinkedIn provides analytics on how many times my posts have been seen.

Scrolling down a bit under your LinkedIn profile, you'll see a section called "Analytics." Click on "Update Impressions," and you'll see your top-performing updates in the last 7 days, 14 days, 28 days, 90 days, and 365 days, along with their counts. Here's a quick breakdown of my previous 90 days of posts.

- **2,000-5,000 impressions: 36 posts, 46 average likes, 8 average comments**

My posts were mostly interactive and engaging with

followers, with 21 prominent posts featuring photos, 8 text-based posts, and 7 video posts. Based on my analytics, photos of my daily life are the most popular.

In my case, I am also known for my "latte series" and "lunch walk series," where I post photos of my favorite coffee. Everyday photos that resonate with users can be a great way to grow your follower count on LinkedIn, as long as you don't go overboard.

Whether it's a photo of your flight to a business meeting, a photo of you and other users at an event, the possibilities are endless. Be confident and try out different types of posts.

- **5,000-10,000 impressions: 11 posts, 80 likes on average, 14 comments on average**

My most significant percentage of posts were text-based posts about career concerns and current challenges: nine out of 11, or more than 80%. This is a considerable number that shows that LinkedIn users prefer this format. Even among influencers with relatively small followings, the ones with more than 100 likes are the ones who regularly post these empathetic and insightful posts.

One influencer who is an executive at a large company has over 600 likes because he consistently posts insights about work life and leadership that he's learned over his career.

You may want your posts to be accessible and infused with experience and expertise. Your posts are also more likely to resonate with your audience if you're honest without exaggerating. If you've been on the fence about writing your first post, it's time to try it.

- **10,000 - 20,000 impressions: 3 posts, 150 average likes, 20 average comments**

My top three posts with more than 10,000 impressions were a tragic event that I experienced, a new record of 85,000 impressions in one week, and thanking LinkedIn users.

From the above analysis, you can see that while an effective posting strategy is essential, the absolute number of followers you have is also crucial to engaging more users.

Embracing the Weird

One of the reasons I was so popular on LinkedIn was that I was willing to try different things that other people hadn't done before. Here are some of my favorite posts:

- **Hip-Hop Fashion Series**

I'm a white t-shirt, jeans, and a baseball cap kind of girl, but I like to post pictures of my daily life on the weekends to connect with people working or taking time off.

My best-performing post in the last 90 days contained 2,719 views, 49 likes, and 29 comments.

You'd think LinkedIn would be all about sharp suits and dapper looks. Still, LinkedIn users loved how I was dressing informally.

- **Metaverse Walking Series**

There is a lake park near my workplace. I walk around it during my lunch breaks for exercise almost every day except during extreme and inclement weather conditions.

One time, I took a video of myself walking in the rain and posted it. One comment said, "It's like walking together in a Metaverse." That comment fueled my post's popularity, and in turn, it became one of my best-performing posts, with 2,764 views and 36 likes.

- **Latte Series**

When I go to a cafe after lunch or on the weekend, I often enjoy a latte or cappuccino, and I like to post about it. For many of us, coffee is our favorite way to relax and relieve stress.

My best-performing post in my "Latte Series" contained 3,149 views, 45 likes, and 12 comments.

Coffee with latte art is popular as it's beautiful to look at and evokes good flavors.

- **Generative AI Series**

At the height of ChatGPT's popularity, I posted images of my avatars and AI models created with various generative AI tools.

4,184 views, 64 likes, 39 comments

I also put up a poll with fun images of me as a movie star, astronaut, etc., and it was very popular with users.

- **My LinkedIn friend made me a character**

- by Screena

Mindset for reaching 10k on LinkedIn

- **It's OK to be human!**

There's a lot of psychological pressure on LinkedIn to look professional. However, I've had followers reach out to me in comments and messages to tell me why they follow me, and it's because I have a "human" touch.

I often brag about my professional and personal accomplishments or share my emotional struggles. Because people on LinkedIn are "people" with feelings, I've found that many can relate to and support me in my ups and downs as a professional and individual.

I post pictures of my casual weekend outfits, coffee at my favorite cafe, or just walking around and saying hello during my lunch break. I have a lot of followers who can relate to my daily life, so I post about them often.

Writing about your family and favorite hobbies in your bio is also a great way to connect with other users. Don't be afraid to show your human side as much as your professional side.

- **Ordinary for me, amazing for others**

Everyone on LinkedIn has a career or is currently running a business. This is why most people forget about the uniqueness of what they do; what you're doing now seems mundane and ordinary. However, one of the most common messages I've received on LinkedIn is the following:

"What you do sounds really interesting. Can you tell me about what you do?"

Consistently posting photos from meetings, business trips, and events will give followers an intuitive sense of what you do. You'll attract followers from all walks of life who are curious about your professional world. Doing so will also give you a good image as a professional and focused person.

Another reason why it's important to be proactive in reaching out to people in adjacent but different professions and fields is because it gives you confidence.

People in your industry have heard about and experienced your work countless times; the "magic" of it has long since worn off for them. However, people in different industries will consider you to be in an exciting world to them. If you confidently explain what you're doing to them, you might get a response like this:

"You're doing something really cool!"

- **Just keep swimming**

In the end, the fastest way to reach 10,000 followers is to keep posting and applying every week. At one point, I went through a period where I was clearing out dormant accounts, and I was losing 100 followers a day. At the time, I was discouraged because I thought people were unfriending me because they weren't interested in my posts or because I was posting in the wrong direction. But once I realized that it was just a matter of cleaning up dormant accounts, I kept expanding my network of domestic and international investors, IT engineers, and people in charge of going global.

It took me about two years to reach 10,000 followers. I wish I had started posting from the start of my LinkedIn journey, but in the end, it's all about consistency. I made a point of liking other users' posts that resonated with me, replying to comments on my posts, and continuing to build relationships with people I had already connected with. After all, LinkedIn is a people-powered space, and interacting with users is a great way to get to know them better.

So, before the week starts again, reach out to as many people as possible. If you get rejected? There are still tons of people on LinkedIn waiting to connect with you.

Who are "Homo Dongmicus,"
"Rapper," and "Ms. Sarada"?

Comments and support from the influencers and followers you interact with on LinkedIn are always a bright spot in your day. My connections have given me nicknames for my hard work and posts, which have become a part of my LinkedIn identity. These nicknames, which show my personality or are based on parts of my name, have become valuable assets I hope to keep with me for the rest of my life.

- **Homo Dongmicus, the fast-acting newcomer**

On LinkedIn, I'm known for my ability to complete tasks quickly. This is one of the reasons why I've been able to increase my LinkedIn following rapidly and why I've been able to expand my presence as a creator. That's why Homo Dongmicus, which means "a rookie with a lot of speed," is one of my favorite nicknames. And on a side note, this nickname inspired this book's title!

- **Sarah Choi, rapper**

I got this nickname because of my penchant for wearing a t-shirt, jeans, baseball cap, and sunglasses. I frequently listen to hip-hop and follow my favorite rappers.

- **Salad Killer, Ms. Sarada**

I eat healthy salads for breakfast and lunch on weekdays, and I've gotten a lot of social media love for my salad eating and food photos. I also started posting on

LinkedIn to encourage healthy eating, which is how I got my nickname. It's a fun nickname that is a variation of my English name.

Goal: Get 10,000 followers
on LinkedIn

Now that you've gotten over 5,000 followers, the next mountain to climb is the 10,000 mark, which I've reached at the time of writing.

While some influencers aren't particularly concerned with growing their follower count, I'm one of those who think this absolute number is very important. However, it's a combination of numbers and influence that will make you an authentic influencer and get you recognized.

An influencer who had done 150+ coffee chats told

me he met someone with over 5,000 followers on LinkedIn. However, he was disappointed because that person didn't seem to have a robust network or professionalism.

Since I'm an average working professional and don't stand out, I diligently applied for connections and posting, and that's how I reached 5,000 followers. I realized that what I needed to do to get 5,000 followers was to just be myself and post without being self-conscious.

But something was missing. I always felt like I was missing that one thing that would make me stand out and become a real "influencer."

In the next chapter of this book, I'll share the last key factor that makes me an influencer with you.

Part 4.

Sarah
the Creator

Cater to your strengths

Unlike other social media, LinkedIn is a business-related social network, and many users on the platform have more than one area of expertise. Like me, many of them are highly motivated to expand their knowledge through content on LinkedIn and use it for personal development or to gain additional expertise. Let's take a look at how I became a creator. It will definitely give you a boost of confidence.

French Food: My Inspiration

I've never been much of a writer. I'd heard of people who painted at 70 and became famous or went to college at 50 and became professionals in their fields, but I never thought I could be one of those people.

I once wrote a book report in school and received praise for it, but I wasn't very good at writing papers, and I mostly read and didn't write. But one day, I saw the movie *Julie & Julia.* It is based on a true story about a woman who wanted to be a writer and blogged about her challenge to cook 500 recipes from a famous French cookbook in 365 days: buying her own ingredients, cooking them, and sharing them with people. Through her efforts, she became a famous author because of the mass following she gained.

I watched the movie and thought:

"I could do that too."

In fact, I have an excellent track record of helping startups raise investment through marketing and PR. The biggest reason why I wasn't able to market myself was because I didn't have my own content or product. But *Julie & Julia* opened my eyes to the possibility of producing the content I experienced in the startup space.

The very next day, I started a blog and wrote my first article.

My first article is published!

- **Defining a startup from an investor's perspective**

What is a startup?

The term "startup" was first used in Silicon Valley, USA.

I had the opportunity to drive the CEO of a global accelerator (early-stage investor in startups) to a startup event. He was busy talking and texting with domestic and foreign investors, large corporations, and startups on his three cell phones. I was nervous I wouldn't be able to ask him the question. So, I cautiously asked him a question during a lull in his phone calls.

"I know a startup established two years ago is already approaching $360K in annual revenue. I've been advising them it's time for aggressive expansion, but the CEO is not considering it. Is there anything I can do to persuade him to scale up the business?"

He said firmly.

"That's not what we call a 'startup'."

I was stunned to hear that a company with $360K in revenue in two years and steadily increasing domestic and international sales was not a startup. The CEO continued.

"We call a company that grows more than 30% in a year a 'startup,' and we only invest in companies with that kind of future potential and vision."

My company holds weekly pitching sessions for startup discovery and supports more than 100 companies a year through various programs. I support dozens of startups a year. Still, I had yet to get this simple concept into my head: only a small percentage of startups are actual startups in the eyes of investors.

A startup is a dynamic company that can grow and increase its valuation rapidly. The term 'startup' was coined by investors looking for a high return on their risky early-stage investments.

Secrets of fast-growing startups

I have another story with an investor. I arranged an investment meeting to introduce the founder to an investor. The meeting went smoothly, including discussions about R&D and sales plans. Still, after the meeting, I heard the following sentence from the investor as a reason for withholding the investment.

"We can't change the CEO's mind."

The rapid growth of a startup is driven by the founder's big vision and goals, and investors are probably meeting with tons of startups today to find them. Let's take a look at the numbers to see how many startups have such a vision:

According to the '2020 Survey on Startup Status of One-Person Enterprises' published by the Ministry of SMEs, it takes an average of 2.5 months for a startup to generate revenue for the first time. According to the' Business Operation Plan in the Next One Year' survey conducted among the same startups, 88% of them planned to maintain their current business operations, while only 6.3% planned to expand their business scale in the future.

Once they've achieved their initial goals, entrepreneurs want to keep their businesses scale. The CEOs don't find a reason to grow any further because they didn't have big plans in the first place. And they become conservative in maintaining the revenue they've already earned and their current operating profit. Only a small percentage of startups ever reach for bigger goals.

As you can probably guess by now, this 6.3% are likely to be the startups that will become unicorns (companies that are less than 10 years old and valued at $1 billion or more), and they'll be led by CEOs with high goals and vision from the start. You can see how difficult it is to identify promising startups and why there are so many articles about the investors who founded these unicorns.

*

The first article I wrote made me a writer, a columnist, and a global thought leader. Even though I didn't come from a writing background, I did it! You should turn on your laptop right now and write about something from your professional perspective. The world that is familiar and sometimes too mundane for you may be entirely new for someone else and something they are curious to take a look at. Let's look at how I grew as a content creator.

Who reads my articles?

When I had about 2,000 followers on LinkedIn, I started writing and posting one weekly article on Blog. I only had 150 "neighbors" on the Blog then. However, there was an excellent analytic function on it.

It was helpful to see the exact number of times and periods that the link to my post was viewed. This data analysis feature provides detailed data such as LinkedIn, the Blog, Mobile-PC, gender, and age group to obtain information about the people who read my posts.

My early articles, viewed 300 to 1,000 times, were read

mainly by people in their 30s and 40s and were viewed on mobile in investor group chat rooms and on LinkedIn.

I also tried posting on other social media sites where office workers gather, but I saw little success. Currently, I'm focusing on promoting my articles in two places: investment and startup-related group chat rooms and LinkedIn.

Me? A columnist?

One day, after writing one article a week, I got a call from a journalist I knew who specialized in startups. He said he'd seen my recent posts on social media and suggested I write a startup column.

"What? Me? Wait, let me think about it...."

At first, I refused, but I realized that opportunities come and go in the blink of an eye, so I said "yes" because I didn't want to have any regrets in the future.

I was a bit scared and nervous that I would actually

be published under my own name in an online media company instead of a blog. However, I had readers who responded to my articles, and some even sent me small gifts as a fan of my articles. So, I gathered my courage and started writing columns about startup movies and posting them where my readers were. And guess what?

My articles became the top article of the day for that media company.

As a somewhat anonymous writer, I was encouraged by my friends and LinkedIn followers, who read my articles and encouraged me with their likes and comments. I now have one more profession, 'columnist,' on my LinkedIn profile, and I'm seeing a noticeable increase in acceptance rates when I send out connection requests.

What's next?

After writing about investment, talent, and startup movies, I couldn't think of anything to write about anymore. That's the biggest worry for anyone reading this. Will I be able to write consistently?

As I was pondering this question, I came across a post on LinkedIn that went something like this:

"If you watch the online startup talk concert I'm moderating and write an article about it today, send it to the email below. We'll review it, and those who write good articles will be selected as EO Planet creators."

-CEO of EO Studio, Taeyong Kim

"What? I can become a creator for the EO brand?"

EO is the most popular YouTube channel in the Korean startup industry, with 550,000 subscribers and a global channel with over 100,000 subscribers. EO Planet was the company's online magazine platform.

I couldn't pass up the opportunity to be a creator for one of the most recognizable brands in the startup world, so I watched a 50-minute video, spent three hours working on an article, and submitted it the same day.

I gained two things from this opportunity. It reminded me that there are so many different things to write about with my entrepreneurial expertise, and it gave me a new professional title to add to my LinkedIn profile: EO Creator.

Putting a Voice on a Page

- **Case 1.**

One day, I saw a post about a speech by Klaus We-hage, a Silicon Valley startup expert, speaking at COME-UP 2022, a global startup event. His speech immediately caught my eye, and I sent him a connection request.

After accepting, Klaus gave me his messenger ID. He asked me to call him, probably because he saw that I was working in the startup field.

He told me the Korean version of his book *Global*

Class, a Wall Street Journal bestseller, would launch this year. After messaging back and forth, I bought the English version of the book and read it, but I only got in touch with him for a while because I needed more time to do an interview.

Then, one day, during the Lunar New Year holiday, I received a message from Klaus:

"Happy Lunar New Year!"

I realized that holding an interview was inevitable. We chatted for a while on voice talk, and although I was terrified, a promise is a promise, so I scheduled an online meeting for our interview.

With the questions I prepared, I recorded the online interview and later transcribed Klaus' voice through the app. Transcribing Korean interviews into articles is relatively easy, but this one took over three times as long. I finished the piece and uploaded it to EO Planet. The result?

It was a hit. It was the #1 article of the day across the platform for several days and received my highest number of date views.

- **Case 2.**

I oversee domestic and international investor relations for the startups in the company. Sometimes, I am asked to attend global IR events in Korea through LinkedIn. Once, I participated in an international investment event organized by KOTRA (Korea Trade-Investment Promotion Agency) and exchanged business cards with people from Canada.

I was introduced to Will Fan, CEO of Emobily, an EV(electric vehicle) mobility company. I told him what I was doing, and he immediately showed me his LinkedIn and messenger QR codes and told me to connect with him.

A closer look at his LinkedIn profile revealed that Will Fan is a global influencer who has been a TEDx speaker, a G20 Canada representative, and an entrepreneur and investor who exited through an IPO (initial public offering) in his 20s.

Despite his illustrious career, Will Fan was calm and humble. He is currently an advisor to an entertainment startup in South Korea.

Soon after, I requested an online interview with him, which became another insightful article. We continue to keep in touch through LinkedIn. I support him through likes and posts as he continues to be an active entrepreneur and speaker.

Micro-influencers have between 1,000 and 10,000 followers,
slightly more than an individual.
They are characterized by their expertise, passion,
and authenticity in a field. Despite their small numbers,
they have a close relationship with their followers
and understand their target audience.

People started calling me an influencer
when I reached 5,000 followers on LinkedIn,
and that's when I started getting opportunities
to try out different content.

Part 5

Branching Out

Say what?

Entrepreneurship speakers are actually one of the hardest things for startups to find. I didn't expect to be asked to speak at one of these events because the most qualified people were entrepreneurs who built successful companies.

Focusing on the spirit of challenge, I spoke about going from an ordinary office worker to a global content creator at a small startup seminar.

I told the story of my journey, which started with finding my unique strengths and wondering how to stand out amongst fierce competition and be recognized by my company.

The audience was mainly startup entrepreneurs, but there were also office workers. I still can't forget the look in the audience's eyes after my talk. Some of them asked to connect on LinkedIn, and I still keep in touch with them.

I can't thank them enough for listening to my story.

Don't forget to tune in!

You know how the saying goes, "An apple a day keeps the doctor away."? Well, for me, "a movie a day keeps the doctor away." As you know by now, I am a voracious movie-watcher. In fact, I've seen over ten movies about entrepreneurship and investing, and I've been able to turn my hobby into an article that's gotten quite a bit of traction.

I've written a series of columns on entrepreneurship and investing, including a movie about how McDonald's became the franchise empire it is today, a story about the founding of Facebook (Meta), a series about a CEO's false business plan that left investors and others in financial ruin, and a movie about the founding of a global coworking space.

I used to send links to these articles to friends and acquaintances until a local station announcer I knew saw them and invited me to be a guest on her radio program. My written content was finally turned into an audio format and broadcast over the airwaves.

I would highly recommend writing your own short written content about anecdotes, books, and experiences related to your field in a way that even a layperson can understand.

Scouting Opportunities

In the last two years, the global startup investment market has frozen over. For this reason, startups are finding it harder and harder to get funding than ever before.

The phrase "cold weather" has started to appear in the media, and seminars have been organized on how startups can overcome this situation.

Since I have always been interested in M&A and foreign investment, this was an opportunity for various forms of startup investment to emerge.

From an investor's point of view, now may be the right time to invest, as company valuations are lower than before, so I started writing articles to share the opinions of experts on various strategies for attracting investment, such as business plans that appeal to investors and focusing on generating sales in addition to R&D.

These well-timed articles quickly became favorites and helped me become known as an expert in the investment world.

I've always loved the startup space, and I've always paid attention to startup investment trends to make sure that the startups I incubate are doing well. That's why it was a great moment for me to see my experience as an expert in early-stage startup investment come to light and be recognized at the right time.

I'm Your Biggest Fan!

The biggest buzzword in the startup world right now is 'global.' The best part about being a LinkedIn Influencer is that I get to connect with investors and startup professionals from all over the world.

When I wasn't sure what role I could play in going global, I found co-authors of Global Class who gave me a lot of insights into what a startup should do when considering going international through real-world company examples.

One day, they contacted me, saying that they were

publishing a Korean version of their book in September and needed to connect with various startup personalities and organizations in Korea.

"Can I... help?"

I hesitated for a moment, but then, I created a list of key people associated with startup organizations and companies. To my surprise, many were already connected to me on LinkedIn, so I could send them direct messages. This was the moment when my professional network finally shone through. In line with the global trend, most organizations, companies, and industry celebrities agreed to meet with the authors.

In the run-up to the book launch in Korea, they organized seminars and talks on globalization strategies, and I was able to contribute three articles to a leading startup media with the authors' insights on going global.

Becoming a Startup Promoter?

While looking for a topic about startup investing, I attended a seminar where a famous startup CEO spoke about financial modeling. When I learned the company was involved in startup investment, I immediately asked for an interview.

The CEO explained as best he could. I took careful notes and wrote an article about the strategies that lead to a startup's investment.

I published the article on EO Planet and shared the link on LinkedIn, social media, and investors' chat rooms. Then, I heard that the article had generated a lot of buzz among investors and startups.

The CEO contacted me afterward and asked me to write more content related to investing and entrepreneurship.

I'm still getting requests for writing articles from companies I'm incubating or have met.

It was a great moment to realize that I was being recognized by an influencer in the startup world.

Reaching 10,000 followers

I'll never forget the moment I saw the number 10,000: It was the culmination of two years of hard work.

As you may have noticed, I didn't just focus on increasing my numbers; I also created a lot of content to fulfill the "creator" designation given to me by LinkedIn. Along the way, I've befriended and collaborated with many influencers and helped them grow as influencers.

The number of comments and likes on my posts started stabilizing, and I'm now averaging 30,000 impressions in 7 days. Of course, that's because I'm still working on it.

In addition to my 10,000 followers on LinkedIn, I have 5,000 followers on Facebook, 4,000 connections on a business app, a community of over 1,000 investors, and a life science community of over 10,000 people, so I'm active in a network of over 30,000 people.

I used to go on LinkedIn and saw many people with inspiring careers. I felt envious and sometimes discouraged by how accomplished these people were. But now, I'm actively interacting with them.

When I reached 10,000 followers and posted about it on LinkedIn, nearly 200 people "liked" the post and a LinkedIn friend drew a celebration webcomic and sent it to me.

I was the joy of tears when I received congratulations from my LinkedIn friends and others.

Now that I've established connections in the startup world on LinkedIn and have expanded my network of domestic and international experts. It's time to start thinking about how to use this network more extensively.

I'm just a regular person working at a non-profit foundation. But now, I've become known as an "influencer" and "startup expert" who is often asked to collaborate with big names in the industry.

It's important to remember that if I can do it, anyone can do it. It only took me two years to reach 10,000 followers.

Keep reaching out to people in your field of interest. Over time, you'll find more and more great people. And they will inspire you to do more.

I also encourage you to post short pieces of written and photographic content that show your expertise. You'll find that having so many people cheering you on will boost your confidence and make you more motivated.

It's an exciting journey, and I'm sure you'll see yourself as an influencer with 10,000 followers before long.

- **Congratulatory image from Ara Koh on reaching 10,000 followers**

- by Ara Koh of W+EAST Creative Studio

Through my LinkedIn journey, I have met
countless influencers in various areas of expertise.
These influencers never cease to reach out to
their followers with heartfelt articles and posts.
By exposing their vulnerabilities, they have become
my go-to people when I'm struggling.
I want to introduce some of the influencers
who have selflessly helped me along the way.

Part 6.

Inspirational
Interviews

• Tyson Junho Moon

Tyson is known in the LinkedIn community
as the "LinkedIn Sage," "Master of Character Creation,"
and "Sweet Guy." He is a favorite among
many LinkedIn users for his consistency
and real-life insights from his 18 years of
engineering experience. His story of going through
240 interviews to get a job
after immigrating to the United States was viral.

🎤 Tell us a little bit about yourself.

I have 18 years of experience as an engineer and have worked in various manufacturing areas such as LCDs, solar cells, OLEDs, semiconductors, and process management and improvement. I am currently working at Samsung Semiconductor in Austin, Texas.

🎤 What made you decide to start using LinkedIn?

I first used LinkedIn for job hunting after immigrating to the U.S. During this process, I used my LinkedIn network to land a job. I learned much about the power of online networks and personal references. Maintaining and growing your network on LinkedIn is very crucial for many reasons.

I'm on LinkedIn primarily to grow my network, which will further my career and help me launch my own business in retirement. To achieve that, I'm building my personal brand by connecting with people through my written content.

How have you found LinkedIn useful?

LinkedIn provides many industry news and updates, especially if you are at an innovative company like a startup or work in a field sensitive to the latest industry trends.

The best thing about LinkedIn is that it provides many networking opportunities with people in your industry.

LinkedIn Learning also offers users a variety of professional development programs that improve personal and professional skills.

You can also use LinkedIn to share your industry information and trends or share your skills and know-how to position yourself as an expert.

Personal branding through LinkedIn can lead to all sorts of offers and opportunities in the future, and you'll often see examples of this through your posts.

🎤 What makes a successful LinkedIn post?

You first have to know yourself before you think about what to write.

Instead of asking, "What are my strengths? What am I good at?"

Ask yourself, "What experiences do I have that differ from others? What unique thoughts do I have?"

The answers to those questions will tell you how you stand out from others, and that's when you can start writing your first post.

On the other hand, when you're commenting on a post, your interest in the other person should come first.

To comment from the heart, you need to at least get a sense of who the author is, their interests, and what they're posting about. If you can do that, you'll be on the path to connecting with them.

At first, it can be as simple as "Congratulations," "I enjoyed your post," "This is encouraging," or "Good insight." Start with a one-line comment like that, and as you get more comfortable, you can increase to two- or three-line statements or even longer.

Finally, coffee chats are more involved. But just like comments, you should prioritize your interest in the other person. Genuine curiosity will help you think of questions and continue the conversation when you meet online or in person.

 Tell us about your most popular posts.

My most popular post was from my "240 Job Interviews" series: "What I've learned from applying for 243 jobs and getting rejected 240 times in the last five years." It had 14,000 views, 173 likes, and 27 comments.

Another popular post was a poll asking, "Who should pay for the coffee in a coffee chat?" which got a lot of interest and engagement. It got 3,900 views, 36 likes,20 comments, and 252 votes in the poll.

 What's been your most memorable experience on LinkedIn?

I connect with people through coffee chats, especially when I see people I've supported and given advice to succeed in getting a job or when they post for the first time and become active on LinkedIn. It feels like a close friend finding success. I look forward to continuing to build on the incredible connections I've made through coffee chats. I hope to continue to be a force for good.

- Ho Yoon

Ho Yoon specializes in global green businesses
(carbon credits, electric vehicle charging, etc.) and market entry
in Myanmar. He is nicknamed the "Master of Coffee Chats"
on LinkedIn. He has been inspiring
and motivating LinkedIn users with posts
about his experiences in the workplace
and interactions with people in various fields.

🎤 Tell us a little bit about yourself.

I have worked at SK for 16 years, including 14 years in trading and 2 years in the sustainability business. In March 2023, I founded my company, Cosmos Bridge Trading, which is engaged in trade brokerage, sales, and marketing business in Asia. I am also working on overseas expansion and investment as an advisor at a climate tech startup.

Based on my six-year experience as an expat in Myanmar while working for a large company, I co-authored "The Real ASEAN from an Expatriate's Perspective" and wrote the Myanmar section.

🎤 You've been nicknamed the 'Master of Coffee Chats.' What does that mean?

I began connecting with people in my industry on LinkedIn to discuss industry trends and started posting those discussions with photos.

Later, I expanded my meetups to include people from other industries and started writing a series of Coffee Chat stories about my experiences. I've posted over 150 stories to date.

By doing so, I've created a new identity on LinkedIn as a "Coffee Chat Storyteller" and continue to build relationships with LinkedIn users.

🎤 Why is LinkedIn good?

LinkedIn is a social platform designed for professionals in various fields. Unlike other social networks, it attracts individuals who seek valuable connections and personal growth.

One of the most excellent benefits is the ability to connect with individuals from diverse professional backgrounds worldwide, including business professionals and office workers, and to share my career experiences with others. I'm currently experiencing a wider world through this platform than ever before.

🎤 How do you make the most of LinkedIn?

Keep sending connection requests to increase your number of connections. No matter how good your posts are, they will only be effective if seen by many people.

It's also essential to frequently respond to the posts of users you've connected with, commenting on them and showing empathy and support.

For example, after someone accepts my connection request, I send them a quick message to say thank you and introduce myself. It takes little effort, and I'm surprised many people don't offer those little gestures. I encourage you to do the same - it makes a big difference.

Finally, it would help if you got over your fear of putting yourself out there online. I only did a little social media before joining LinkedIn. Taking a small step of courage to post and respond to others' posts leads to more connections, bringing me new information, knowledge, and insights, as well as new opportunities to engage with my connections.

🎤 What are your most popular posts about?

My most popular post was a message to those starting out on LinkedIn: "Take a leap of faith." It received 15,000 views and 270 likes.

My most viewed post was "Coffee Chat with Google's Lead Designer and Author," when I talked to someone who has appeared on a TV show and has a large LinkedIn following. The post received 17,000 views and 220 likes, and I realized that influencers can be very effective.

Also, my article '4+1 Things I Did to Dream of Independence While Working a Job' received 17,000 views and 220 likes, which resonated with many working people.

What has been rewarding
about using LinkedIn?

I've met people from all walks of life, industries, and roles on LinkedIn. It's meaningful to connect not only with the big names in the industry but also with ordinary people like me.

Through my identity as a passionate Coffee Chat storyteller, I'm most proud that I'm contributing to revitalizing the Coffee Chat culture in Korea, where conversations with strangers are relatively unfamiliar. I feel rewarded when I receive responses like, 'I'm enjoying your Coffee Chat stories,' 'I can relate to your story because it's similar to mine,' and 'I find courage, support, and inspiration in your posts.'

• Yuri Kim, Coach

Yuri Kim has an extensive career
with international schools across China, Vietnam,
and Malaysia. She has rededicated her job as an educational
and positive psychology coach and mentor.

She shares her life stories through witty and sincere posts,
offering comfort, encouragement, and support.
Her posts resonate with many LinkedIn users
navigating professional and interpersonal challenges.

🎤 Tell us a little about yourself.

My international journey began back in 1995 in Tianjin, China. Over the years, I've ventured to various countries, including Perth, Australia, Ho Chi Minh City, Vietnam, China, and Malaysia. At the same time, I have 22 years of experience as an international school teacher and leader, supporting both students and colleagues.

I am an International Coach Federation accredited coach and hold certification as a Positive Psychology Specialist. My passion lies in supporting teenagers and their parents as well as adults as a coach and mentor. Additionally, I conduct workshops for parents within the international school community.

🎤 How do you utilize LinkedIn?

I use LinkedIn to connect with professionals from diverse fields, not only within the international school community but also to gain more information and expand my knowledge in my professional area.

It is rewarding and valuable to know that my posts and comments can uplift other LinkedIn users. Additionally, I look forward to sharing more about my new coaching and mentoring business, which will lead me to future opportunities to grow my business.

🎤 Why LinkedIn?

LinkedIn is a platform where individuals from diverse professional backgrounds converge with the common themes of "career" and "work".

LinkedIn is not just about career development but also community development. Users share advice, offer support and encouragement, and cultivate mutual growth and mutual support, which adds value.

Currently, I am broadening my horizons by connecting with professionals in various fields, providing me with the opportunity to explore new perspectives in different worlds.

🎤 I want to make the most of LinkedIn,
how can I do that?

You can resonate with LinkedIn users by sharing your unique story as your content. It is also important to strategically increase the number of connections.

An essential part of this process is the principle of "Give and Take" - it's important to help others grow while you grow yourself.

By liking posts that resonate with you and actively interacting with them through comments, you can increase your followers. At the same time, you can build great relationships with them.

🎤 Can you tell us about some of
your most memorable posts?

My post, "When I feel negative emotions," received 12,980 views, 118 likes, and 48 comments. In this post, I provided simple, practical tips on how to deal with negative emotions in our daily lives, drawn from my own experiences. This post resonated with many individuals.

Another memorable post combined the theme of "Celebrating 10 years in Malaysia" and "Coffee Chat Review," attracting 5,613 views, 153 likes, and 80 comments. I am pleased that I could highlight the value of networking by sharing my personal experiences.

🎤 Can you share your future plans?

I want to expand my educational coaching and mentoring center under my personal and business brand, EduchologyPlus+. At the same time, I aim to make meaningful contributions to educational institutions worldwide and public education systems in Korea. In particular, my goal is to empower teenagers to reach their full potential as valuable members of society.

These educational programs can encompass academic, emotional, and mental support.

Additionally, I aim to promote educational programs that prioritize mutual respect and cooperation among family members, fostering happier families in line with the slogan "Happy Parents, Happy Children."

Looking ahead, I aspire to take on the challenge of publishing my own book. Moreover, I want to give back to the community through initiatives such as webinars. By sharing our experiences together, I hope to create a space where we can provide mutual support, encouragement, and personal growth together.

Little did I know that two years of social media use
would allow me to get to know so many people,
work on projects with others, and build friendships.

In this final chapter, I'd like to introduce you to some
people I'm grateful to have connected with on LinkedIn,
who have helped me work on focused projects and
discussions that have opened my eyes to various
industries and new fields.

Part 7.

Oh, the People You'll Meet!

Entrepreneurs

• TaeYong Kim

- YouTube Creator and CEO of EO Studio
- EO Studio is a media company that promotes startup entrepreneurship worldwide with a simple vision: "The World Needs More Entrepreneurs."
- 22,000 followers on LinkedIn

Two years ago, I couldn't have imagined that social media would be the gateway to connecting with outstanding individuals like TaeYong Kim. He's not only the CEO of EO Studio but also a startup content creator.

His 22,000 LinkedIn followers are a testament to his influence. I vividly recall the excitement of becoming a creator on EO Planet, thanks to one of his LinkedIn posts.

After becoming a popular creator on EO Planet, I met TaeYong at a party. I remember being thrilled to meet someone famous in the startup.

Known as the forward to his future endeavors as he continues to inspire countless entrepreneurs through global entrepreneurship beyond Korea.

• Klaus Wehage

- Co-author of the Wall Street Journal bestseller "Global Class"
- Co-Founder & CEO, 10X Innovation Lab
- Trained, advised, and spoken to over 3,000 executives in over 50 countries based on his work at the Silicon Valley Forum and the 10X Innovation Institute
- Known as the "Silicon Valley Ambassador" for turning the struggling non-profit "Silicon Valley Forum" into a global success
- 15,000 followers on LinkedIn

Klaus Wehage, co-author of the Wall Street Journal bestseller *Global Class*, came into my LinkedIn network when I sent a connection request after an eye-catching post at a global startup event.

Known as the "Silicon Valley Ambassador," Klaus has a knack for helping startups expand globally, and his 15,000 LinkedIn followers reflect his expertise.

The biggest buzzword in the Korean startup scene is "global." Connecting with an expert from Silicon Valley, the heart of the startup scene, means a lot.

His insights into how startups go global will surely advance the Korean startup industry. His globalization insights will energize and transform the Korean start-up scene.

• Will Fan

- Founder & CEO, Emobily
- TEDx Speaker
- G20 Canada Representative
- 6,000 followers on LinkedIn

I met Will Fan, a Canadian serial entrepreneur and TEDx speaker, at an investor relations event by KOTRA. After initially exchanging business cards, I looked him up on LinkedIn. I realized he was an accomplished CEO and investor who had already experienced an IPO and startup exit in his 20s.

Emobily, a company that develops urban micro-mobility, such as electric scooters, has been recognized as a promising startup by Microsoft and won an award at the 2035 E Mobility Taiwan Global Demo Day.

Despite his illustrious career as an entrepreneur and investor, Will's humble and sincere demeanor left a lasting impression on me, and we look forward to seeing what he can do for a sustainable future. Will Fan is a name to watch in the ever-evolving landscape of entrepreneurship and sustainability.

- Co-author of the Wall Street Journal bestseller *Global Class*
- Professor at UC Berkeley, Haas School of Business
- Serial entrepreneur with three successful exits, founding companies in a variety of industries, including FinTech, mobile, e-commerce, and real estate
- Selected as AT&T's youngest regional vice president (27 years old) and a recipient of the AT&T Diamond Club (top 1% of sales managers globally)
- 10,000 followers on LinkedIn

I had the pleasure of meeting Aaron McDaniel at the launch of the Korean version of Global Class.

As a professor at UC Berkeley, Haas School of Business and a seasoned entrepreneur, Aaron has experienced an inspiring journey from FinTech to real estate. He once was a contestant on the American TV Show "Shark Tank."

I'm excited about the mentorship and guidance he'll continue to provide to Korean startups aiming for global success, as he has demonstrated tangible success within the industry.

• Bokkee Lee

- Founder & CEO, Wanted Lab Inc.
- A professional executive who led Wanted from a startup to a listed company.
- Wanted Lab Inc. is an AI-based HR technology company that provides recruitment-matching services and career-related content utilizing AI technology. Startups make up a significant portion of its customers, making it a crucial player in the startup ecosystem.
- 3,000 followers on LinkedIn

I spoke with Bokkee Lee, co-founder of AI talent-matching company Wanted Lab Inc., at the "Wanted-C Forum: Go Global" event at the Google Startup Campus.

He is an entrepreneur with a successful startup IPO and is currently pivoting towards globalizing the company's services.

I remember how frank he was about the difficulties of this venture to go global with the company.

I also wish Wanted Lab Inc. success in going international.

• Ara Koh

- CEO of W+EAST Creative Studio
- Illustrator of Lotte World's "Lotty Friends"
- Produced webtoons for Incheon Airport Railway, the National Agricultural Cooperative Federation, and various Korean government entities.
- Art director and Project Manager for "Sheepfarm in Meta-Land" Art Director and co-founder of "Sheepfarm in Sugarland"

Ara Koh

Ara Koh, a trailblazing individual with incredible success, is creative and selfless. W+EAST Creative Studio collaborates with colleagues, crossing the boundary between digital and reality. The company is determined to push the boundaries in global business and creativity.

Ara has garnered this distinct following through the refreshing medium of webtoons. She is a talented creator creating a lot of buzz on LinkedIn with her 'InkedIn' webtoon series. Ara is now an influencer of influencers.

She commemorated me with a personalized webtoon when I reached my 10,000 followers milestone. I look forward to seeing her continue to bring out LinkedIn users' creative sides.

• Ken Kwangjung Kim

- CEO of Screena
- users can watch and enjoy OTT content together while chatting in real-time and also operates synculab, a specialized distribution platform for virtual assets.
- Metaverse & Blockchain expert
- Advisor for Sandbox's "Woo Youngwoo Metaverse Project"
- Web 3.0 Platform Influencer: 5,000 followers on Link3, 6,500 followers on Phaver

Ken Kwangjung Kim

I first met Ken Kim through the NFT Study Group, a community learning service run by his company, Screena. Professionals in the Metaverse field and creators involved, including the film, webtoon, drama, and animation industries, learn to utilize blockchain technology. Blockchain technology and metaverse allow for the interaction between many creators in this niche community.

He is very humble and actively shares his insights to help people prepare for changes in the world.

I look forward to seeing him continue to serve as a thought leader in the industry to make the Web 3.0 world more accessible to the general public and enable content providers to build innovative businesses based on blockchain and metaverse.

• Andy Woojin Kim

- Co-founder & CEO, Business Canvas
- London School of Economics and Political Science (LSE) International Management Master of Science (MSc)
- Business Canvas is a company that builds software that solves problems faced by B2B companies. Its products include Typed, a document collaboration tool, re:catch for sales modeling, and Typed Finance for financial modeling.
- 3,800 followers on LinkedIn

Andy Kim is the CEO and co-founder of Business Canvas. I initially met him through social media and had the opportunity to meet him in person at a seminar focused on startup funding strategies.

In an era where sales and financial modeling have assumed paramount importance in navigating investment challenges, his company, Business Canvas, emerged as a novel player. Business Canvas is recognized for hosting some of the most captivating online events within the Korean startup ecosystem. It garnered considerable industry attention for its innovative approach to startups experiencing investment "cold spells."

I anticipate that Business Canvas will continue to make a substantial positive impact on the startup ecosystem, ushering in fresh perspectives and opportunities within the global startup landscape.

• Gordon Dudley

- Founder & CEO, RDI Worldwide
- RDI Worldwide is an HR specialist providing global recruitment services for Korean companies with offices in Korea and overseas.
- 20,000 followers on LinkedIn

Gordon Dudley is the founder and CEO of RDI Worldwide, an HR specialist company providing global recruitment services for Korean companies. With offices in Korea and overseas, RDI Worldwide connects Korean talent with new and tempting opportunities worldwide. In addition to Gordon's professional career, he is passionate about providing HR services to Korean startups.

I had the pleasure of meeting Gordon at Next Rise, Asia's largest startup exhibition. Since then, he's become a LinkedIn influencer known for his HR insights videos, often shot while strolling through the vibrant streets of Gangnam. Gordon's entrepreneurial journey and dedication to his work have earned him a substantial following, making him a valuable resource for the startup community.

Life Science
& IT Experts

- Dae Wook Lee (Medicine)

- Medical Director and Medical Franchise Head of CV&GTx, Department of Clinical Development & Medical Affairs, Novartis Korea
- Graduated from Warwick Medical School, UK
- Graduated from Harris College of Business (Faulkner University) Executive MBA, USA
- Rare Disease International (RDI) WHO virtual consultation advisor (Korea Representative)
- 2,800 followers on LinkedIn

Dae Wook Lee is a super-dad and super-worker who cherishes his time with his twins and is a loving husband - all while trying to expand his career in the medical field.

Through LinkedIn Live, he generously shares his many career pivots - from attending medical school in the UK to working at a global pharmaceutical company.

He has a warm heart and encouraged me whenever I struggled with staying true to my aspirations for my career. I look forward to his positive influence and guidance towards others.

- Dr. Siyeon Rhee

- Medical Director and Medical Franchise Head of CV&GTx, Department of Clinical Development & Medical Affairs, Novartis Korea
- Graduated from Warwick Medical School, UK
- Graduated from Harris College of Business (Faulkner University) Executive MBA, USA
- Rare Disease International (RDI) WHO virtual consultation advisor (Korea Representative)
- 2,800 followers on LinkedIn

Dr. Rhee is an instructor at Stanford University School of Medicine and the Co-Founder of K-BioX, a vibrant bio community boasting over 10,000 members worldwide. Dr. Rhee is among the most passionate community organizers I've ever seen. Dr.Rhee has taken it upon himself to create dynamic connections within the bio-academic and tech world. I first crossed paths with Dr. Rhee six years ago while I was working on a biotech video project. We later fell out of touch, but our connection was rekindled through LinkedIn a year ago. This year, he organized the K-BioX SUMMIT in Korea.

Dr. Rhee is a pure and passionate community organizer, ensuring that K-BioX remains a thriving hub for students and professionals in the biotech industry. His efforts hold the potential to connect talented individuals from around the world with Korean biotech companies, bolstering the growth of the life science industry.

- Diko Ko

- Senior Software Engineer, Moloco, a machine learning-based advertising solution IT company
- Founder & COO of Singta Inc. Altwave Lab, Inc.

Diko Ko, a senior engineer at AdTech company Moloco, sat next to me on a plane flight eight years ago when he was en route to an Apple conference.

He used to run a game company and now works for a company in Silicon Valley called Moloco. On LinkedIn, he blogs and posts about the company's growth and the cultural events in his personal life.

When he visited Korea, he took the time to chat with me and share the latest accomplishments and successes of the company. I look forward to hearing more about his experiences with Moloco.

• Seunghwan Lee

- Author of "The Birth of Super Individuals Who Will Never Be Replaced in the Age of AI"
- National Assembly Future Research Center
- Adjunct Professor, Hanyang University Business School
- National Assembly Future Research Center
- Research Fellow at the Samsung Research Institute

Recently, while thinking about the skills needed in a world increasingly dependent on AI, I found a post about Mr. Lee's book, "The Birth of the Super Individual." I liked and commented on it, and after being deeply compelled by the now-bestseller, I asked for an interview, and the humble Mr. Lee graciously accepted.

That interview led to one of my most popular articles, in which he shared many profound insights about adapting to this rapidly changing world. His perspectives are invaluable, and I am grateful to have had the privilege to learn from him.

Lee's intuitive and easy-to-understand explanation made his articles very popular. I look forward to reading more of his insights to help us prepare for the rapidly-changing future.

- Jaeseung Kim

- Principal Researcher, Corporate Research Center of Pion Electric Co.
- A master of LinkedIn comments
- Influencer in a world of followers
- 1,000 followers

I first met Jason at a seminar for startups looking to enter the business industry in the Middle East.

With an impressive command of LinkedIn, Jason has become a micro-influencer as he garners countless followers.

His unique worldview, sharp wit, and engaging comments set him apart as a distinctive follower whose popularity continues to grow among smaller users and influencers alike.

I eagerly anticipate witnessing more of his insightful work on LinkedIn.

Global Startup Ecosystem Builders

• Jihye Kim

- Managing Director of Strategic Finance, SparkLabs Korea
- M&A, Strategic Planning/Investments at CJ E&M and SM Entertainment
- Deal Advisory at KPMG, Seoul
- Financial Accounting, Valuations and Regulations at Deloitte, New York

Jihye Kim

Jihye Kim is an accomplished professional with a diverse background in finance and strategy. Jihye currently serves as the Managing Director of Strategic Finance at SparkLabs Korea, where she plays a pivotal role in shaping the financial landscape of the organization. Her journey to this role has been marked by significant milestones, including experience in M&A, strategic planning, and investments at renowned companies such as CJ E&M and SM Entertainment.

I met Jihye Kim at Maru 180, a startup incubation center. Jihye brings her wealth of experience and financial acumen to the startup world, where she focuses on managing investments, strategizing for growth, and navigating complex economic landscapes. Her extensive background and current role at SparkLabs Korea aid her as she continues on the path to catalyzing startup success and driving growth in the startup ecosystem.

- Julie Youngju Choi

- Program Lead at Tenity, a global startup accelerator in Singapore
- Program Manager, K-Startup Center Singapore
- Exploring and nurturing Korean and global startups seeking to scale up and expand globally, with a particular focus on their growth journey in Singapore
- 2,000 followers on LinkedIn

I first met Julie on LinkedIn while working at K-Start-up Singapore. She is now a Program Lead at Tenity, a global startup accelerator headquartered in Switzerland. Julie provides invaluable guidance and support to Korean and international startups aiming to expand their market presence in Singapore and Southeast Asia.

This year, our paths crossed once again at NextRise, one of the most significant startup events hosted annually in Korea. Julie's magnetic personality and her unwavering commitment to the startups she collaborates with leave a strong impression on others around her in the same industry.

I look forward to watching her success in the thriving entrepreneurial landscape of Singapore, a globally renowned hub for innovation and business development.

• Jonathan Moore

- Chief Innovation Officer, Pentaflow

- Co-founding Partner, Next Stage Studios

- Mentor/EIR at Techstars and 500 Global

- Seoul Honorary Citizen

- Host of Podium Star, South Korea's most prominent
  English pitch event

- 6,000 followers on LinkedIn

Jonathan Moore has been a key figure in South Korea's startup ecosystem for over a decade as a founder, connector, and mentor. At Pentaflow, he leads the development and execution of innovation programs aimed at fostering startup growth, attracting investments, and facilitating global expansion.

He previously co-founded one of the EdTech startups, and he oversaw marketing at a Korean unicorn startup. Recently, his work has resulted in 50+ Korean startups achieving major innovation awards, thereby contributing to the elevation of Seoul's global ranking in the startup landscape.

We've been following each other's activities on LinkedIn for a few years. I recently connected with Jonathan on LinkedIn for advice on international investments and investor relations.

• Daeyeon Jin

- Product Manager at WRTN Technologies
- Business Development of APAC region for Silicon Valley tech companies (Evernote, mmhmm, Chegg, Awair, etc.)
- Managed Carrot Letter and Fanssastic Community for productivity
- Author of "Giving Wings to Evernote" and "Reverse Thinking Trends 2023"
- 1,400 followers on LinkedIn

I met Daeyeon at a global startup event. As a Product Manager at WRTN Technologies, a generative AI company, his work spans diverse areas.

He's worked with Korean startups like Flow, Allganize, and Collabee and has been a helpful resource, contributing to their growth.

Dave is not just a project manager; he's a multifaceted professional managing the newsletter Carrot Letter and the Fanssastic community.

His contributions are instrumental in nurturing the Korean AI and tech industry as well as other various related communities.

• Riso Dongok Ahn

- CEO, The Garrison
- Startup Grind and Foreign Entrepreneurs Club community
- Runs Cross Border Startup Ecosystem Builder Forum
  with the Korea Accelerator Association
- 1,500 followers on LinkedIn

Riso Dongok Ahn

I first met Riso Ahn at the Entrepreneurs Night event. He recognized me as a LinkedIn influencer and greeted me warmly. Riso Ahn is vital in fostering a global eco-system for Korean startups.

He collaborates with various organizations and companies to run programs for foreign entrepreneurs through his business, The Garrison. The Garrison is more than just a coworking space; it's a startup consult-ing company dedicated to empowering foreign entrepre-neurs.

Riso is also involved with Startup Grind and the For-eign Entrepreneurs Club community. In a world where startups need diverse networks to expand globally and attract overseas investments, Riso's contributions are vital.

I look forward to our continued collaboration in sup-porting startups.

• CJ Yoon

- Founder & CEO, Forward
- Forward provides consulting services to help overseas companies enter the Korean market and develop their businesses.
- Seoul City Lead of Global Class
- Startup mentor of Founder Institute

CJ Yoon is the founder & CEO of Forward. This consulting company assists overseas companies in entering the Korean market and developing their businesses. He's also the Seoul City Lead of Global Class and a startup mentor of Founder Institute.

I first connected with CJ at a seminar on globalization strategies. His extensive experience in e-commerce, SaaS, and healthcare made him a sought-after mentor and speaker at startup events.

As the Seoul City Lead of Global Class, CJ is crucial in spreading the culture of global entrepreneurship in Korea and fostering a thriving global ecosystem.

Content Creators

• Jinny Jiyoon Kim

- Editor, EO Planet
- EO Planet is an online webzine run by EO Studio

Jinny Jiyoon Kim

Jiyoon Kim, an Editor at EO Planet, a thriving online webzine under the management of EO Studio, has been a pivotal influence in my journey as a contributor. Her impact on the platform is undeniable, boasting an impressive track record of over 10,000 article views.

When I applied to be an EO Planet creator, I had the privilege of being mentored by Jiyoon, who adeptly coached me in crafting captivating article titles and composing engaging content.

I remember writing new articles and sometimes wondering, "Should I have posted this article?" and doubting my skills and final product. Jiyoon's consistent engagement with my posts on LinkedIn gave me the courage to continue my passion for writing articles.

• Jeremy On

- College Consultant at Taiwanese startup 'Pano Education'
- Experience in M&A, Venture Capital, EdTech
- Work experience in four different countries (the US, Singapore, South Korea, and Taiwan)
- Ringle Tutor
- Graduate of Emory University - Economics, Mathematics, and English major

Jeremy On

Jeremy On, who now works at a startup in Taiwan, first met me on a 1:1 English tutoring app called Ringle. With a Korean father, Jeremy is familiar with both Korean and American culture, so he can make concepts easy to understand and relatable.

Aside from teaching English, he's also an editor who gives my English articles great titles, so he's a great friend.

He has voiced his desire to start a career in software engineering, and we have worked together to increase his LinkedIn presence.

It has been an absolute pleasure to watch him grow from a university student to a working professional over the past few years. I know that he will continue to do great things in the future.

- Yunjoo Shin

- EO Planet Editor
- EO Planet is an online webzine run by EO Studio

Yunjoo Shin

Yunjoo is a creator on EO Planet and frequently engages with users on LinkedIn through its commenting and liking features. Yunjoo and I (along with another editor, Jiyoon Kim, and CEO Tae-yong Kim) met twice last year for advising sessions on how I would like to direct my future toward my passion: writing.

It was so nice to attend a startup party and meet her for the first time in person.

Despite the challenges I've faced, the encouragement from the EO team has consistently motivated me to keep writing. The EO team combines content skills with humility, creating a supportive environment for writers like me to keep connecting with kind-hearted people like Yunjoo. Even though I've gone through some lows at times, I've always gotten back on my laptop with the encouragement of the EO team and the platform's contributors.

I look forward to utilizing the platform and seeing its expansion in the future.

- Brasley Byun

- SAP Student Training And Rotation Intern
- Curiosity Project Team, Jeongsu Scholarship Scholar
- Winner of the 2019 Chung-Ang University Book Debate Competition
- 3,000 followers on LinkedIn

Brasley Byun

Inspired by notable LinkedIn influencers, Brasley Byun embarked on a journey of sharing his experiences and pioneering spirit with fellow users. My initial encounter with Brasley occurred over a coffee chat, and it was immediately apparent that he is an authentic and genuine person.

He revealed that, even during the most challenging moments, he discovered solace and motivation through engaging with people on LinkedIn about his honest experiences. Today, Brasley has become a source of inspiration for many, igniting motivation for both work and life through insightful posts about his professional journey and personal posts about his daily experiences.

I eagerly anticipate witnessing his success, both as a consummate professional and as a prominent LinkedIn influencer.

Global
Networking
Professionals

• Hyun Chai Lee

- Head of Scaled Growth Enablement (SGE)
- Former Head of APAC DSP Business at Moloco
- Accounts Management & Partnerships at Google, Meta, etc.
- Extensive experience in IT solution sales in Asia
- 3,700 followers on LinkedIn

Hyun Chai Lee

Hyun Chai Lee is a senior director at Moloco. Moloco is headquartered in Silicon Valley and was founded by Koreans.

Hyun Chai landed this position because of his extensive experience in IT solution sales across Asia. Currently, he leads SGE at Moloco and previously worked as the Head of APAC DSP Business.

I first encountered Hyun Chai when he gave an enlightening talk on corporate globalization strategies at Moloco's Korean office. His insights were invaluable, and I was impressed by his ability to connect me with contacts in the startup media industry.

I look forward to hearing more of his advice and insights on how startups can enter the Southeast Asian market.

• Christopher Lai

- Current Director of the Hong Kong Trade Development Council (HKTDC) Korea Office
- A quasi-governmental organization established to promote global engagement with Hong Kong, Asia's financial hub and gateway to global business.
- 6,600 followers on LinkedIn

I first connected with Christopher Lai through LinkedIn. Since then, he has successfully connected experts from Hong Kong's financial sector and other startup organizations.

He has one of the largest working networks of anyone I know, and his multidisciplinary knowledge of finance and trade makes him an excellent resource for entrepreneurs looking to go global and attract overseas investment.

He has organized events in various fields, like the biotech and fintech industries, for cooperation between Korea and Hong Kong. His commitment to furnishing startups and companies with information and networking opportunities makes him a catalyst for international growth.

- Josh Kim

- Partner manager at G-P(Globalization Partners) Korea
- G-P is an HR tech unicorn startup offering services in 187+ countries.
- Strategic partnerships & alliances in Korea, Japan, and China.
- Expat Manager (Daekyo Shanghai / Hong Kong)
- Global Sales / Partnership Manager (Daekyo Group)
- 2,700 followers on LinkedIn

Before his current position, Josh Kim gained experience working in Hong Kong and Shanghai, where he established a substantial network in B2B sales and partnerships. This network has proven invaluable in his current role, enabling him to facilitate connections between the two domains.

Josh took the initiative to request an online coffee chat, which served as the catalyst for our discussion on expanding G-P's HR solutions services in Korea.

His extensive knowledge of global business and networking makes him a valuable resource for startups looking to grow and thrive globally.

- Andrius Sankauskas

- Current Commercial Counselor at the Embassy of Lithuania in Seoul
- Former Commercial Counselor, Embassy of Lithuania in China
- Helping Korean biotech startups enter the European market Promoting Lithuania as a gateway for Korean biotech startups to the European market
- 2,000 followers on LinkedIn

Andrius Sankauskas is a dedicated commercial counselor at the embassy of Lithuania in Seoul and a former commercial counselor at the embassy of Lithuania in China. Andrius is on a mission to assist Korean biotech startups in entering the European market. He tirelessly promotes Lithuania as a gateway for Korean biotech companies seeking to establish themselves in Europe.

I had the pleasure of meeting Andrius. And, he shared invaluable insights into Lithuania's incubation policy for biotech startups in stem cell and gene therapy. His work involves connecting Korean startups looking to enter Europe with bio institutes and attracting foreign investments to Lithuania.

We're actively exploring various partnerships to facilitate the growth of promising Korean startups globally.

• Jong Choi

- CEO of M3 Global, LLC
- In charge of Global LAVA Korea
- Former KOTRA Los Angeles & Chicago Trade Representative
- 1,500 followers on LinkedIn

After getting to know him through a casual online coffee chat, Jong Choi and I decided he was a perfect fit to lead my startup entry into the U.S. market. We organized a webinar for biotech startups on entering the U.S.. And, we scheduled an investor relations event for U.S. venture capitalists.

His experiences in consulting at KOTRA Chicago and Los Angeles led him to found his own company, M3 Global LLC. He is also the Korean representative for the L.A. Venture Association. He is actively involved in revitalizing the startup ecosystem in the L.A. area, including biotech. He has the potential to lead cooperation with investors, venture capitalists, and startup incubators in the U.S.

I look forward to working with him as a bridgehead for companies to successfully enter the U.S. market.

Epilogue

Many people on LinkedIn are professionals or entrepreneurs looking to grow their own professional brand as well as their company's brand. LinkedIn is an excellent platform for people who constantly strive to develop themselves as professionals, to keep up with industry trends, and to gain the skills to apply to our evolving working world.

If you're only connecting with people you know in your industry, it's time to expand beyond that and join LinkedIn.

Good information comes from good people. Don't miss the opportunity to connect directly with a wide range of talent in your industry and adjacent fields.

You'll get a good idea of where you stand, whether you're ahead of the curve, and if you still need to learn more or gain more experience. You can get real-time feedback from hundreds of people who can help you determine your areas of improvement.

I've expanded my network of companies and celebrities in my industry by persistently reaching out to them. I've connected with them directly, which has helped me significantly increase my knowledge and connections quickly.

While 10,000 followers may seem like a lot, you can become a micro-influencer with just 1,000 connections by being selective and focused. You can spread your voice across the platform and engage with your followers.

The biggest thing I've gained from this platform is the ability to confidently introduce myself to people in the startup world and beyond, referencing my established position as an influencer.

In the past, when I had an idea, I would come up with excuses to not act on it or delay action. Now, I make sure to "go for it," and most of my attempts have succeeded.

If there are any of you out there who have been thinking about posting but haven't gotten around to it because you're nervous or afraid, I want to encourage you to just try.

As I've shared from my own experience, just one post a week that demonstrates your subject matter expertise is all it takes to be seen as an influencer and an expert in your industry. I want to challenge you to write your first post today.